STORIES OF THE GREAT WAR

Eileen Boland

Comprising

STORIES OF THE WAR
1915

MORE STORIES OF THE WAR
1915

CATHOLIC TRUTH SOCIETY

PUBLISHERS TO THE HOLY SEE

War, with all its horrors,
is lightened by the instances
of devotion and sacrifice which
always emerge from an otherwise
tragic and terrible record.

Eileen Boland was married to CTS's General Secretary.

CTS ONEFIFTIES

Originally published as *Stories of the War* and *More Stories of the War*: both 1915.

Published by The Incorporated Catholic Truth Society,

40-46 Harleyford Road, London SE11 5AY

www.ctsbooks.org

Copyright © 2017 The Incorporated Catholic Truth Society.

ISBN 978 1 78469 538 5

STORIES OF THE WAR

Mrs John Boland [Eileen Boland]

STORIES OF THE WAR

It is some consolation that war, with all its horrors, is lightened by the instances of devotion and sacrifice which always emerge from an otherwise tragic and terrible record. The war now being waged has already supplied an abundance of such material, gratifying not only to Catholics, who note the heroism of priests and nuns, and the religious revival in France, with special pleasure, but also to those "other sheep" of the Christian flock who have written and spoken with so much sympathy of these things. Out of this abundance the following pages have been compiled; they relate some of the many stories which throw into vivid light the power of Faith to serve the cause of Fatherland. We begin with a few instances of work accomplished by

Priests in Action.

"Eighty-seven Catholic priests and 127 nuns have been awarded the Legion of Honour by the French Government for the services rendered to troops in the field of action." So says the *Times* (December 4th) within four months of the outbreak of the war of 1914. We have not all the details of the heroic acts which earned this distinction, but enough has been published to show that the priests have followed, in the letter and in the spirit, the instructions of the Bishop of Poitiers: "Before all and above all be a priest; that is, a man of duty among your heroic brothers in arms. By word and example raise their hearts to God. The reputation and honour of the clergy of France are in your hands; it is your duty to preserve this treasure and make it at once more glorious and greater." How well the priests have succeeded, the Paris correspondent of the *Times* shows: "One result of the war has been a distinct religious revival in France. The so-called clerical peril has disappeared from the popular imagination in the face of the real peril of the German invasion. Everywhere the priests have been distinguished for their heroism, and their devotion to the patriotic cause is shared by many members of religious orders, both men and women. Abbé Luchat, a sergeant in a cyclist corps, was killed on the field of battle, after having been mentioned in dispatches on the previous day. Abbé Monbru, a lieutenant of infantry, fell at the head of his company. Another clerical lieutenant, Abbé Grenier, was struck down in leading his men in a charge. Abbé Fumin, an ensign, died also in battle. In the imperishable roll of soldier-priests figure twelve abbés who were either officers, non-commissioned officers, or private soldiers.

"The *Journal Officiel* contains the following lines, typical of the gallantry shown by French priests in the present campaign: 'Abbé Buscoz, adjutant of the 97th Infantry, has died as a hero. He had just been promoted a second lieutenant on the field of battle for two acts of bravery. His last hours were admirable. He dashed to the attack with his men, while crying, "I am a priest; I fear not death; *en avant!*"'" (October 2nd).

Another *décoré*, the Abbé Lamy, a priest-sergeant of the diocese of Amiens, continued fighting and looking after his men in spite of five bullet wounds. When unable to walk, he crawled about to assist his wounded comrades in arms, giving them brandy, and, as a priest, ministering to them the consolations of religion (*Tablet*, October 24th). Sergeant Lemoine, a priest of Bourges, himself wounded, rescued his officer from among the dead amid a storm of bullets and carried him to safety (*America*, November 21st). Another priest-sergeant, the Abbé Féval, of Vandré, offered himself for service at the front in place of a father of a family of five children.

Mgr. Ruch, Bishop Coadjutor of Nancy, and Mgr. Perros, Vicar Apostolic of Siam and Titular Bishop of Zoara, are both in the French Army, the latter as a sub-lieutenant.

French Jesuits and their Work.

Members of religious orders, too, are sharing in this fine work. "There are at the front 99 Jesuits from the Province of Paris and 183 from the Province of Lyons; 144 French Jesuits exiled in England have returned to their regiments; 12 have been killed and 20 wounded. The Rector of the French Jesuit College at Jersey is at the front" (*Stella Maris*, December).

A correspondent comments thus on the position of these returned exiles: "I met a Jesuit the other day on sentry go. He had been in Canterbury for years. 'Curious,' he said; 'I was expelled from France as a Jesuit. Now I come back to fight for her.' 'Curious, do you call it?' I replied; 'I call it magnificent.'"

Studies for December gives the following story of one of these priests, modestly veiled under the initial "de G.," as related in a letter from a chaplain:—

"I have just heard the confession of a man, when another calls me: 'Father, give me absolution!' 'Most willingly,' I answer, hastening to his side; 'but what has happened to you?' 'Well, the truth is, my thigh has been broken by a shell; but let me tell you how I came to be carried in here. A comrade did it, who is a soldier and a priest like yourself. A fine fellow he is! If you only knew what he has gone through for us! He would rush through a hail of bullets to lend us a helping hand, without seeming to notice the danger he was running. To tell you the truth, Father, after he had saved me and placed me here, I threw my arms round his neck and kissed him!' 'Where is he?' I asked. 'Gone back to the firing line,' he replied. 'And what was his name?' 'His name is de G.' At the sound of that name all the poor fellows around joined in: 'That's a man for you! He's more than a man, he's a hero. Talk about bravery—and then the way he worked for us without a thought for himself. No one will ever know, Father, all he has done for us.'"

In another letter the following is told apropos of the same Jesuit: "You may, perhaps, have heard of de G. He has just received la médaille militaire et la citation à l'ordre du jour of his regiment, both on the battlefield and in the depôt of Montpellier. Five reasons were assigned for the award. It appears that the officer who read the dispatch in the barrack-square at Montpellier paused and said: 'Those are excellent reasons. Who is this M. de G.? Does anybody know him?' A soldier (a Benedictine) replied, 'I know him; he is a Jesuit priest!' Tremendous applause on the part of all the soldiers."

"Died Hand in Hand."

An unnamed priest is the central figure in this story from the *Daily Chronicle* of October 31st:—

"In the hall of a great railway terminus in Paris a number of wounded were laid out on the straw waiting to be taken to a hospital. Eight of them were very badly hurt, and some of them were evidently not long for this world.

"One of them seemed to be very uneasy. A nurse went up to him and offered to rearrange his bandages. His reply was, 'I want a confessor very badly.'

"'Is there a priest here?' asked the nurse.

"Just then another soldier lying mortally wounded plucked the nurse by the sleeve. 'Madame,' he said, 'I am a priest; I can give him absolution. Carry me to him.'

"The nurse hesitated. The soldier was suffering from the effects of a horrible shell-wound, and the least movement gave him excruciating pain. But again the feeble voice quietly said, 'You are of the Faith, and you know the price of a soul. What is one more hour of life compared with that?' And the soldier raised himself by a supreme effort to go to the side of his comrade.

"But the effort was in vain. He had to be carried. The confession did not take long, and the strength of the soldier-priest was ebbing rapidly away. When the time came to give the absolution he made a sign to the nurse. 'Help me to give the sign,' he said.

"The nurse held up his arm while this was being done. Death followed quickly for the soldier-priest and his penitent. They died hand in hand, while the nurse and the ambulance men fell on their knees on each side of them."

A Priest-Volunteer.

The death of the soldier-priest Emmanuel Demoustier took place on the battlefield of Arras. "Towards evening on October 3rd, the ammunition was exhausted owing to the violence of the struggle. The captain of Private Demoustier's company asked for a volunteer to warn the supply convoy, and in making the request he did not hide the fact that the mission was a dangerous one. Père Demoustier offered himself at once, and before leaving said to his neighbour: 'If I do not come back, take what is in my bag.' Then he set out bravely. Struck by a shell on the way, he fell not far from a captain of artillery who was riding by. He had the strength to give him a pencilled note. Half an hour later the ammunition arrived and the fight went on. Père Demoustier died in the night. His noble action was mentioned in the order of the day to the Army" (*La Liberté*, December 16th).

A *Times* correspondent describes the following scene which he saw at a wayside station in France during the battle of the Marne.

"The train stopped. Those of the men who could walk descended and were helped to food, which, with the tenderness of women, they carried to their stricken comrades in the wagons. The village curé arrived. He began to work with zeal, helping his brave compatriots. Suddenly a soldier ran to him and touched him on the arm. The good man's face became very grave. He followed to one of the wagons, where a little crowd had gathered. In the wagon one of France's brave defenders was even then giving up his life. It was a strange and terrible moment under the cold moonlight, and with the sound of the cannon still audible away under the hills. The clergyman pronounced a brief blessing. The wounded man's arms, which had been crossed upon his breast, fell to his sides; his breathing ceased. One of the nurses broke into tears" (September 14th).

The Antwerp correspondent of the *Morning Post* (September 10th) tells how "at Rouen the men, wearied in spirit by the trials through which they passed, were inspired with fresh courage by an old priest. This priest, who had fought in the war of 1870, has a little church at Petite Couronne, which was Corneille's village, just outside Rouen. On August 28th, when the Belgian soldiers arrived, the abbé assembled them in the forest, and at a drumhead altar conducted divine service to music by the band of the 10th Regiment, which, having lost its own instruments in the retreat, used others borrowed in the village. The men recall now with tears in their eyes that solemn service in the wood and the sermon of Abbé Lemire. They say that such an ardent flame of patriotism and courage burned in his eyes and lifted his voice from out the feebleness of old age, making it ring like a clarion, that their souls were lifted up and their spirit renewed."

Not to men of their own faith alone do the priests bring help and comfort. Gunner C. Ayres, of the 29th Battery R.F.A., quoted in the *Evening News* (October 2nd) says:—

"Not long before the ambulance chaps took me away I was surprised to hear close in my ear a gentle voice half-whispering to me. As the figure came round my feet into the line of vision I soon made out the cloak and hat of a kindly-faced priest. He knelt down by me, and, heedless of the shrapnel still flying round, said what I could easily guess were a few short prayers. Then in very poor English he asked me if I was ready to die, and, quite honestly, I was. He then opened my shirt and took out the metal disc which gives my number and name on it, and attached to the cord a little cross with the Virgin Mary stamped in relief upon it, and said, 'Blessed for you by Pope.' Soon after that the ambulance came. Nothing will ever lead me to believe other than that the priest saved my life. I can only think that after leaving me he saw the Red Cross men and directed them my way. I like to believe it, anyhow. Although I am Church of England myself still the Christian acts of these brothers of the Cross prove them to be made of all the right stuff."

The Priests of Belgium.

Here is a tribute to the Belgian priests:—

"Some way back I notice a stationary group by the way-side. I approach and find that its centre is a dying man, who has been taken from the cart that was bearing him from the field and placed tenderly on the bordering grass. Kneeling by him is a priest, holding one of his hands and administering extreme unction. On the edge of every battlefield I have seen these ministers of God. Whilst the fighting is going on they move about, calm and fearless. Each wears around his hat a narrow band of the Belgian colours and on his right arm a Red Cross. They are ready to help the doctors or to comfort the last moments of dying soldiers" (*Daily Telegraph*, September 30th).

Is it any wonder that an Irish Protestant, speaking of the Belgian priests to Mr. Hilliard Atteridge, said: "I could not imagine braver or better men. They were up to the firing line, and whether you were Catholic or Protestant didn't matter. They never asked, but just set to work to save your life. I am an Irishman, and I was a Protestant until Mons. But their religion is the religion for me, and I have put my name down to be a Catholic" (*America*, November 14th).

Of the bitter sacrifice these deeds of heroism may entail we get but glimpses here and there.

"The other day a wounded soldier was brought into hospital and it was found necessary to amputate his right thumb. It was impossible to administer an anaesthetic, yet the wounded man bore the operation without a groan. When all was over, and the surgeon was about to pass on to the next case, the soldier burst into sobs. 'What?' said the surgeon kindly; 'you did not even wince under the knife, and now when it is all over you are crying!' 'That's not the reason,' replied the patient; 'I am a priest, and amputation means that I can never say Mass again'" (*Daily News*, November 23rd).

Faithful to their Posts.

It is wonderful to see the heights of bravery and devotion reached by non-combatants, clergy and laity alike.

"In certain towns, as at Luzarches, only the parish priest remained. The priest installed himself at the Mairie and became mayor and gendarme, issued safe-conducts, received staff officers, and courageously represented all the absent. All this gave an idea of a fearful upheaval, which was bound to make an impression on the soldiers."

A *Telegraph* correspondent writes from Pontoise: "I walked to the church, where the bells had been ringing, and where I gathered from the religious chant that a service was being held. To my surprise there were only three persons to form the congregation. The clergy were all alone around the altar and chanted the *Te Deum* by themselves. Nothing ever impressed me so much. Here were the priests, all alone, who had remained faithful to their post to the last and had clung to their duty. Now they gathered round the altar to thank Heaven for their country's deliverance. Outside the church I spoke to one of the few men I met. He was a lonely concierge, sitting at the door of his house, abandoned by all the tenants. 'Have the curés been here all this time?' I asked. 'Yes,' he replied; 'and their presence cheered us up. They said Mass and read the Litanies every day, and that made us feel less lonesome'" (*Daily Telegraph*, September 18th).

"There is one man in Meaux whom the people are idolizing, the Bishop, Mgr. Marbeau. On September 1st, all the officials, including the mayor, left the town, and the more well-to-do of the inhabitants followed their example. There remained behind the Bishop and his clergy and the very poor of the people. The Bishop, working with a committee, has taken charge of the town. He spends his days looking after the wounded, visiting the battlefields, burying the dead—I learnt that the priests themselves have acted as bearers—and caring for the poor people who have been left behind. By the force of his personality, by his unselfishness and his courage, the Bishop has reconquered for the Church in Meaux the position that it used to occupy. The woman I spoke to and others in Meaux look upon him as their friend and saviour'" (*Morning Post*, September 18th).

In a French Château.

A Yeomanry officer, writing from the Château Fontenelle, near the Belgian frontier, says, in a letter printed by the *Morning Post* (September 22nd):—

"You will wonder how it comes that we are in a château instead of fighting in the field. The story will interest you. We are hiding until it is safe to clear out and rejoin the force (French or British) when the enemy has evacuated the country…. Villagers, who eyed us suspiciously at first and were uncommunicative, overcame their shyness at the sight of Englishmen, who carried proofs of their goodwill in the shape of a recommendation from the Cardinal Archbishop of Amiens, who has most kindly issued to several British officers engaged in scouting and reconnaissance duty this most valuable sealed passport to the hearths and homes of Northern France. We were warned to avoid certain places, where the enemy was known to be in some strength, and a schoolmaster on a bicycle took us in the direction of this place, which he knew would be safe. The owner of the château is a widowed landowner, who would not leave her village and people, so I thought it civil to ask the schoolmaster to go on ahead with my card and compliments and explain that if it would embarrass her we would seek rest elsewhere. The reply came to us without delay that 'a most cordial welcome was at the service of the ten soldiers if they would accept the shelter and hospitality of the château.'

"And what a reception it was! The dear old lady is eighty years of age and walks with a stick, her snowy-white hair dressed à la Marie Antoinette. She seemed like a picture on the walls of the Palace of Versailles. Two Sisters of Charity, who were on a visit, attended her as she stood at the entrance to her beautiful castle, secluded in a grove of trees—roses everywhere. I quickly explained our predicament. Was it, I asked, dangerous for us to hide in her barns? 'No, I have remained here because I wished to be helpful.

How can I be more useful in this war than by feeding travellers who have lost their way? Take off your uniforms. My servants will go at once and buy civilian costumes for you,' was the reply. So we all kissed the hand of our benefactress and are resting and hiding until we receive intelligence. The place is off the main route and away from turnpike roads, which explains why the dear old soul has escaped molestation. I have forty pounds in French money, but I dare not ask her to take a franc, even for the clothes she has purchased. The men sleep in a large, roomy barn, and I have a wash-house to myself. Our arms, uniforms, revolvers, and saddlery are under an enormous pile of firewood."

Soldiers' Piety.

Soldiers as well as the clergy have earned fame for their magnificent piety.

A soldier of Marseilles wrote from the Haute Meuse on September 19th:—

"During the fighting at H—— the people had fled before the shells, and the curé, who had gone to visit a sick parishioner, was prevented from returning home. The church was set on fire and I heard le bon Dieu was still in the tabernacle. I told my captain, who immediately ordered me to remove It. Taking the altar cloth to cover It, and amid a rain of debris and shells of all sorts, we succeeded in carrying le bon Dieu to a place of safety. We kept the Blessed Sacrament for a day and a half till the curé arrived and carried It to Verdun."

"The Irish Guards were one day last week the heroes of an incident which has been the subject of enthusiastic comment from one end to the other of the British lines. The famous regiment was ordered to take an exposed German position, and, before advancing, they knelt for a moment in silent prayer. Then, springing to their feet, they fixed bayonets and dashed in wide open order across the exposed plateau, swept by the enemy's machine guns. What remained of the regiment—for many fell—took the German position at the point of the bayonet. Eye-witnesses state that our men crossed the plain hurrahing and singing, while many of them had a look of absolute happiness and joy on their faces" (*Evening News*, September 23rd).

The Last Mass at Vassincourt.

As one of the chaplains says, the war is a great mission and "the German cannon is worth all the missionaries put together."

Private letters and public correspondence alike teem with stories of the return of negligent Catholics to their duties, and of the conversion of sceptics. The difficulty consists not in finding but in selecting incidents. One such typical instance is worth a lengthy extract; it is told by a doctor in the French Army Medical Corps to the special correspondent of the *Matin*:—

"We came one night to the little village of Vassincourt. Hardly had our wagons been put up and our camp pitched before we threw ourselves upon our 'grub' (popote), for everybody was dying of hunger. The cook had not had time to get any fresh meat, so we had to make shift with 'monkey' and tomato sauce.

"As soon as we had finished eating the orderly came and told me that a man wanted to speak to me. It was one of our stretcher-bearers, a brave lad, who had always previously kept in the background.

"'Monsieur le Médecin-en-Chef,' he said to me, 'tomorrow is Sunday. I ask permission to go to Mass at the church here.'

"'You are, then—?' I said.

"'Vicar in my own village,' was the reply.

"'Granted.'

"'Many thanks, M. le Médecin-en-Chef.'

"As soon as he had gone, it was suggested that all the mess should go in a body to the Mass of the stretcher-bearer, and this proposition was carried by acclamation. The other two ambulance corps were advised, and they, too, jumped at the idea.

The Scene in the Church.

"Sunday morning came. As I was the senior officer, the place of honour was given to me facing the choir. My brother officers sat on each side of me, and behind us were the nurses and stretcher-bearers, who came because we had come.

"The officiating soldier-priest entered, and what struck me at first were the red trousers below the chasuble and the alb. But we were in the presence of the enemy, and it was not the time for taking off your uniform.

"I had not been to a Mass that I know of since my first communion, except occasionally at marriages and funerals, but these did not count. And at the commencement I was very uneasy, for I could not remember when to rise, when to sit down, when to bow. But our soldier-priest made a sign to me with his hands what to do, and the others all followed my example.

"Then suddenly our soldier-priest began to speak to us. He told us that there were only soldiers in the church; that all who took part in the Mass were for their country; that many might have stayed comfortably at home, considering their age. And then he suggested that there were many among us who neglected a little the good God and His Church, but who were at the same time serving Him by our work.

"And he added that it was better—not to invoke unceasingly the spirit of the Lord; not to proclaim that He is with us on the buckles of our belts and on the plates of our helmets—but to respect His teachings more, the first of which was to be good to others and not to cut our brothers' throats.

"After that he started talking about our families, about our womenfolk at home consumed with anxiety about us, and about our little ones whom, perhaps, we should never see again; about the example which those of our corps had left us who had died in doing their duty.

Interrupted Tears.

"Then I began to feel something damp running down to the end of my nose. I looked to my right and there I saw our dispenser— you know the old pill-roller, who believes in nothing, not even medicine—making the most horrible grimaces in order to hide his emotion; while on my left the other Médecin-en-Chef was busy scrubbing his moustache with his handkerchief as hard as he could.

"I drew out my handkerchief, and this seemed to act as a signal. Soon other handkerchiefs were fluttering all over the little church. Then some one sobbed noisily; it was Sidi, an old soldier from Africa, who in civil life is the keeper of a square in some part of Montmartre.

"And then just at that moment, as if to enable us to hide our snufflings, the whole building began to vibrate, and we heard music of a kind, which certainly did not come from the organ. It was cannon on all sides of us. We ran to the doors, and the last thing I saw was our soldier-priest giving us a hasty blessing, and then running to the sacristy to put off his sacerdotal vestments and become a soldier once more.

"This was the last Mass for some of those who were at Vassincourt on that beautiful autumn Sunday of 1914. It was also the last Mass at the poor little church in which we had mingled our tears. She also died a soldier's death; she was burnt by the Prussians" (*Daily Chronicle* Paris correspondent, writing on October 8th).

The Story of H———.

"While yet under instruction, H——— volunteered for the front as soon as the war broke out, and was twice wounded fighting near the Meuse. The second time one arm was so badly hurt that he lost consciousness. When he awoke, it was to find himself in a trench at some little distance from another British soldier, who was apparently in a worse condition than himself. H——— managed to reach him by creeping along the ground on his uninjured side. He saw that the man was nearing his end, and asked him if he was a Catholic, but understood that he had no religion in particular. 'Before I came out,' H——— said, 'I learned an act of contrition. Would you like to say it with me?' The act was slowly repeated by the dying man, and with the last word he yielded up his soul to his Maker. H——— now saw a Red Cross ambulance, and endeavoured to sign for help, but he was, unfortunately, espied by one of the enemy's patrol, who did not hesitate to run his sword through the dead man's body and to trample with his horse over H———, thus rendering his condition mortal and leaving him unconscious once more. When he came to himself he was in the cottage of a Flemish husbandman and his wife. Every endeavour was made to save his life, but it was evident that it had nearly run its span. The good folk offered to bring a priest to him, but H——— refused to expose them or a priest to danger. He told them that he was not actually a Catholic, but earnestly desired baptism. 'In that case I will baptize you myself,' his host replied, and forthwith the little room was hung in white and decorated with flowers, and the ceremony was then and there performed. Meanwhile, H——— had given them the address of his brother, who arrived from England two days afterwards, in time to hear the story from his lips and to assist at his deathbed. H—— is buried in the garden of the little Flemish, homestead. Before he died he won the gift of the Faith and the desire to be received into the Church for his brother, who is himself at the front now" (*Second Spring*, December).

Acts of Faith.

Writing to Mgr. Keller, the Rev. W. Forrest, chaplain with the Expeditionary Forces, speaks of the 4th Division, with which he worked:—

"What a good work and what an excellent soil! The faith of the old Crusaders was not in it, and wherever you went and while you remained with these faithful Catholic men, nothing else was anything to them. God bless them all, for they have given me more joy in these three months than the whole rest of my semi-wasted life has given me. It was worth waiting for. It is true to say that the German Kaiser is fighting a community of saints—'converted' if you like—but with not a mortal sin scarcely to be found among them. General absolutions to regiments or very large bodies of men were the order of the day, at least in this division, and men, especially of the Irish regiments, had general absolution two or three times a week" (*Cork Examiner*, December 4th).

A touching act of faith is reported by a young soldier in France:—

"On the 20th of August we were at Morhange, in Alsace-Lorraine. In the afternoon we attacked. The enemy's bullets were whistling in our ears. One of my comrades falls mortally wounded at my side. He calls for a priest. He feels his strength leaving him. It is impossible to procure him one. The poor fellow, making a supreme effort to pull himself together, and steeping his finger in his wound, writes on the ground with his blood, 'I believe in God.' He died a few moments afterwards. I saw the chaplain the same evening; I related this scene to him. He replied, 'You were not the only spectator. This death has made a conversion. One of your friends, who had been very indifferent, was touched by this act of faith of the gallant soldier-lad; he came to confession. For many years he had not seen a priest'" (*Studies*, December).

Here is a picture of Bruges in August, from the pen of an English resident:—

"One of the most impressive sights of this tragic time is that of the incessant crowds of people who tramp in pilgrimage, night after night, along the route of the famous yearly procession of the Holy Blood. They flock on in groups of all numbers, all sizes, from solitary persons to hundreds together: whole parishes come, whole families, all praying as they go—sometimes in dead silence, when nothing is heard save the tramp of feet, sometimes reciting the rosary, and the hum and the roll of the clamouring voices is like the incessant breaking of great waves. Heaven is being besieged" (*Tablet*, September 5th).

Priest-Martyrs of the War.

In this terrible war non-combatants have been in almost as great danger as those actually fighting. "The list of priests who have been killed by the Germans in the bishopric of Namur alone is appalling. The names of 27 priests appear in the list, without taking into account the 12 who have disappeared since the German invasion, with regard to whom information is lacking. In the diocese of Liége six priests have been killed" (*National Volunteer*, Dublin, December 19th).

The following detailed account of the shooting of a Jesuit scholastic was sent to the *Tablet* (September 19th) by one of the Farm Street Fathers. It is based on information supplied by the Belgian Superiors of the Society. The brother of the Father Willart mentioned was in England recently. He had seen his brother and other eye-witnesses of the scene and was able to confirm the accuracy of the account.

"After the burning of Louvain, fugitives of all descriptions, including a large number of ecclesiastics, made their way on foot to Brussels. For the most part they were allowed to enter Brussels freely, but as it was pretended that the priests had been inciting the people to fire on the Germans, the military authorities refused to allow ecclesiastics to pass until they had searched them. Amongst the crowd of ecclesiastics thus lined up and searched on the Tervearen road was a young Jesuit scholastic, a lad of twenty-three, not yet ordained. This student, Eugène Dupierreux by name, happened to have in his pocket a notebook, in which he had kept a sort of diary of the events of the previous few days, with certain comments of his own, in which he compared the destruction of Louvain to Omar's burning of the library of Alexandria, and noted that even the French Revolution had left the University buildings standing.

Sentenced to Death.

"The German officer in command, having found this document, compelled one of the other Jesuit students, who happened to know German, to translate passages aloud. The officers then formed a sort of court-martial, examined the book further, and forthwith sentenced the student to be shot. A cross was made upon his back with chalk to indicate that he had been condemned, and at his own request a quarter of an hour was given him to prepare for death, during which he made his last confession to Father Willart, one of the priests present. He then stepped forward and was placed against a tree by the side of the road. He had told his companions to turn their heads away. 'Ne regardez pas,' were his last words to them, but the soldiers obliged them to look on. A volley was fired, which apparently did not kill him. 'Il trébucha,' says the account of the eye-witnesses, and then an officer stepped up close and put a couple of bullets through his head. A hole was straightway dug at the foot of the tree and the body thrown into it.

"Upon a protest being subsequently made through the papal nunciature at Brussels, it appears that an official inquiry was held and that the higher military authorities decided to court-martial the officer who had ordered the execution. Beyond this nothing is so far known. Robert Dupierreux, the twin brother of the deceased, who is also a Jesuit scholastic, was one of the many ecclesiastics arrested as described and present at the scene. Most of these were afterwards placed in carts and driven through Brussels as a sort of derisive exhibition. Eugène Dupierreux, who was shot, is described as a lad of very gentle character and unusual piety. The pretext for the murder would seem to have been that the notebook was supposed to contain the heads of an inflammatory sermon which the writer intended to deliver; but seeing that he was so young and not yet ordained, he would never have been allowed to preach in public. The obvious conclusion is that the Germans were determined to inspire terror somehow, and that they seized upon the first victim against whom they could discover the semblance of a case."

How the Abbé Délébecque Died.

The following from "a correspondent in France" appeared in the *Times* of September 26th:—

"The Abbé Délébecque, formerly a professor at the College of Our Lady at Dunkirk, who was falsely arraigned as a spy, was summarily executed on Friday morning at Valenciennes. He was returning on his bicycle to his parish at Maing after being present at a memorial service to his father, who died a month ago, when he was arrested by a patrol of Uhlans. He had no incriminating documents in his possession, but was the bearer of a number of letters from French soldiers at Dunkirk to their families. He was tried at midnight by a court-martial composed of officers, who, after the mockery of a trial, condemned him to be shot at daybreak as a spy.

"Confided to the care of a German military chaplain, he passed the night in prayer in one of the waiting-rooms at the station. Having confessed and been fortified with the rites of the Church, he was taken at 5 o'clock in the morning by motor-car to the place of execution at the foot of the Dampierre Column on the outskirts of Valenciennes. The abbé, who throughout showed the noblest fortitude, gave his captors a letter to his mother, and, after telling some of those present that he offered his life for his country, knelt in prayer, and a moment after fell lifeless, pierced by a dozen bullets. His body was afterwards conveyed to Maing, where it was buried by his sorrowing parishioners. This act of piety was owing to a passer-by, the Germans having unceremoniously thrown the body of their victim into a hastily made grave not deeper than a foot and a half. The passer-by, seeing a portion of a cassock protruding therefrom, placed some stones on the grave in the form of a cross, while some women of the vicinity strewed it with flowers. This coming to the knowledge of the Abbé Petiprez, with whom the German military chaplain was lodging, he succeeded with much difficulty in obtaining the permission of the German authorities to exhume the body and to reinter it at Maing.

"The Abbé Délébecque is the seventh priest in the diocese of Cambrai to be shot by the Germans."

At an Aerschot Convent.

The Sisters of the Order of Ste. Dorothée, who have arrived in London from Aerschot, were expelled from Portugal at the time of the civil revolution, and shortly afterwards they started a noviciate in Aerschot. Once more they have been obliged to seek refuge, in

England, and one of the sisters told a representative of the *Tablet* (October 3rd) a graphic story of their experiences in Belgium. It seems that the arrival of the Germans was feared some days before they appeared.

"I went down to the town to shop (said the Sister), and everywhere there was a dreadful atmosphere of expectancy. The people were quite calm, as the Belgians always are, and they stood in little groups in the streets, wide-eyed and with pale faces, talking to each other in whispers. A German aeroplane was sighted and fired upon, and I made my way back to the convent under a hailstorm of bullets.

"The Germans entered the town on the 19th and searched everywhere for Belgian soldiers. They were fairly quiet at first, and the people behaved splendidly. They came to search our house, but I think they guessed they would not be successful, as they did not pursue their search. They then demanded food, and we had to give them all we possessed. We gave them all our bread, butter, and coffee; but when they asked for wine, of course we told them we had none, except our altar wine. They called for this, but it was evidently not strong enough, as they sent a soldier into the town for as much champagne as he could get. As they ate, two Sisters were told to stand by the table to taste everything, in case the food and drink was poisoned! From the 19th of August until the 9th of September they came to our house for everything, and were furious if we did not answer the door quickly or were unable to give what they asked. I myself was obliged to go round the house looking for food, with a soldier following me and pointing a revolver at my head. One evening they came in and ordered that flowers were to be placed on their dinner-table, as it was their commandant's birthday! They told us that the Kaiser was in Paris and that Antwerp was in the hands of the Germans. All this time the cannons kept up an unceasing roar, day and night; and when we asked the officers where it was, they said, laconically, 'Anvers.' Of course it wasn't true.

The Belgians Return.

"On September 7th we saw that a large body of Germans were gathered about our house. They were all looking up the road and were equipped for marching. The sound of firing came nearer and nearer, until we sought refuge in the cellars. We heard a dreadful fight overhead, and this lasted for some hours. At last one Sister crawled to the cellar entrance to see what was happening. She heard voices whispering above, 'par ici, par là,' and came back to say that she thought the Belgians were in the town. At last a Belgian soldier came down and told us that the Germans had been driven out of Aerschot. It was a strange sight to see the poor people pouring down into the town once more. They had been hiding in the woods and hills round the town for three weeks, living on any scraps of food available.

"Although the Germans were no longer in the town we did not hope that they would not return, and we knew that if they did we should receive no mercy, so we got together some little possessions and a tiny bundle to take on our journey. There was a rumour that a train would leave Aerschot for Antwerp, and we ran to the station, which was three-quarters of an hour's walk away, on the chance that a train might go. The uncertainty of it was awful, for we knew that Uhlans were in the woods round the town. We arrived at Antwerp eventually, and then took a boat crowded with Belgian refugees to England. We arrived at eleven o'clock at night, and were taken to the Alexandra Palace, which was crowded with the poorest of poor Belgians. Here we obtained mattresses and blankets. Shortly afterwards we were transferred to the Hackney Casual Ward, where we were given beds. Some soldiers who were quartered there insisted on giving us a concert, and that we should have our photographs taken with them."

Tributes to the noble work of the nuns abound on all sides. A cavalry officer in a letter home which appeared in the *Times* (September 11th) says:—

"I am writing this by the roadside, so excuse writing. We've had the hell of a time. All by ourselves—the English against a force of Germans five times as big. Our troops have been wonderful. I am so dreadfully sorry for the inhabitants. Their villages set on fire by shells, and they running about with their few precious things not knowing where to go. Truly war is a most awful thing. I never realized it before. All the people are awfully good to us.... The convents are grand and the nuns splendid. We were done awfully well by them. We subscribed to one between ourselves."

A British officer in France writes:—

"There have been some fine scenes of devotion and heroism of nuns and doctors tending the wounded when the shells were pounding through roof and wall, scattering lath and plaster and stones far and wide, and almost suffocating with dust those who escaped with their lives. One of the Sisters of Mercy, with a deep flesh wound in her arm, would not let go of a poor dying cuirassier she was supporting with her right arm, and made the doctor bind up her wound whilst she gallantly remained at the bedside of her charge. A priest who had just left the hospital after administering extreme unction to three infantrymen was killed in the vestry of his church as he was putting on his vestments just before Mass" (*Evening News*, October 1st).

A Scottish nun in Belgium wrote on August 7th to friends in England:—

"Since yesterday morning our schoolrooms are cleared of desks and benches; fifty sewing machines, bales of cotton for mattresses, sheets, etc., are piled in the corridors. For two days we nuns on our side have been rolling bandages, tearing linen into squares, triangles, bandages for the head, etc. In our schools alone the committee of the ladies of the town have to provide 150 beds, sheeting, blankets, etc., and there are at least six other centres of the same committee in this town. We gave twenty-five beds, all ready and complete, from the retreat house, and offered our big classrooms to the town for any use they desired. The big Jesuit College has done the same, and, as you know, last week, if you got my letter, the troops were quartered in the Jesuit College on their way to the frontiers.

"Tell father I am cheery, and feel sometimes far too warlike for a nun. That's my Scottish blood. I hope to goodness the Highlanders, if they come, will march down another street on their way to the caserne, or I shall forget I must not look out of the window."

The same brave and warlike spirit animated a Sister of Charity whose story is told in the *Croix*. She was asked by the commander to shut herself up in a fort in order to look after the soldiers in case of need. She asked permission of her superior to take this duty. "But what if the commandant should blow up the fort rather than surrender?" "Why then," answered the Sister, "we shall all go up together, and the bon Dieu will receive us, since it would have been for Him and for France."

The Heroine of Gerbéviller.

But the most famous nun at the present time in France is Sœur Julie of Gerbéviller. Gerbéviller itself has been twice burnt, twice bombarded, and for a fortnight occupied by the Germans. Throughout all Sœur Julie remained at her post as superior of the hospital and has earned for herself a foremost place in the annals of the war. "A month ago," says the Belfort correspondent of the *Times* (September 22nd), "Gerbéviller had 1,600 inhabitants and consisted of 463 houses. To-day there are six left. The rest are nothing but bare, roofless walls, blackened and desolate, gaping holes which were once windows, piles of ruins. Like Jerusalem of ancient times, the town has been reduced to a heap. The Angel of Death has passed over it, and as a habitation for men it exists no longer. Only at one place, right on the outskirts near the station, there are a few traces of human life in the form of wounded soldiers and inhabitants searching in vain for the sites of their houses; and among them an angel of charity and devotion, a solitary nun, Sister Julie, who throughout the occupation by the enemy and the bombardment remained faithfully at her post, healing and encouraging the wounded and the inhabitants. And in the rest of the town, among the ruins of the church and in the houses, even in the streets, a frightful silence."

Saving the Blessed Sacrament.

On entering Gerbéviller, the Germans at once began to pillage the church. They attempted, by firing shots at the lock, to break open the tabernacle, but being unsuccessful, they left the church. Sœur Julie succeeded where they had failed, forcing open the lock by means of a bayonet, which had been left in the sanctuary. She found the sacred vessels overturned and pierced by bullets. Collecting the scattered Particles, she brought away the ciborium and hid it in her dispensary cupboard. Later, fearing discovery and sacrilege, she consumed the Hosts. Meanwhile the town had been fired, and Sœur Julie and the three sisters under her began to fear for the wounded in their charge. "I told the Germans," she said, "that I could not allow them to kill my wounded. They insisted on going all over the hospital, and then they agreed to leave it alone. But I had to protest again, as they wanted to set fire to the rest of the street, and that would probably have meant the destruction of the hospital as well." Eventually Sœur Julie had the German wounded as well as the French to look after—"a hard trial to Christian charity," she says, "but we did it." With the return of the French to Gerbéviller the wounded have been removed, and the nuns, converting their hospital into a bakehouse, still serve their fellow-citizens by baking bread.

Writing at the end of September, a *Times* correspondent visiting the town says: "I saw practically only two things that were whole. One was a stone crucifix, standing by itself at a point where two streets meet, the other the figure of the Virgin with the Child Christ in her arms, looking from her place above the altar down the shattered nave and through the burnt and broken door of one of the churches—and around and above her on every side this abomination of desolation that the German soldiery have left behind them."

On November 29th Sœur Julie was presented with the Legion of Honour, by the President of the Republic himself, "for having by her presence of mind and firmness defended the hospital and provided for the subsistence of the wounded and the inhabitants during the bombardment."

German Catholics: A Story of the Rosary.

In Germany, as well as in Ireland, Great Britain and France, there has been a wonderful religious revival. The Lubeck correspondent of the *Times* on November 23rd describes the religious wave which has swept the country:—

"The Roman Catholic churches, especially along the Rhine and in Southern Germany, are never empty during the day. It is pitiful to hear the quiet sobbing of women in the churches and to see the black dresses. I have never witnessed a more touching service than in Cologne Cathedral one Sunday morning in the middle of October. The priest happened to mention the destruction of the

Cathedral of Rheims and a heartrending sob was heard among the worshippers. There was a long silence, and then the priest knelt down and ended his sermon with a prayer for peace."

Like our own men, too, the Catholic Germans find comfort in the Rosary. *La Presse* relates the experience of some French soldiers who surrounded a farmhouse by night:—

"There was a passage before us, and at the end a door. We could see a faint glow, and we heard low murmurs. Our officer dashed across the passage, with us close behind, and throwing open the door, entered the room. A strange sight met our eyes. We had entered a low vaulted room, lit by two flickering candles placed at either end of a long table. Kneeling round the table were five Germans, three officers and two soldiers, praying. One of the officers held a string of beads between his fingers. We shouldered our rifles and our officer called out to the Germans to surrender.... The officer who held the rosary explained in French that they had lost their way in a storm, and having nothing to eat or drink, had entered the farmhouse to seek food and shelter. They had given themselves up for lost and had knelt down to say a last prayer. He asked our officer if they would be shot, and seemed much relieved when told that they would all be treated as prisoners of war."

The Dying Uhlan.

A member of a Paris *patronage* writes:—

"Sent with five men to reconnoitre in a wood, we came across a Uhlan officer with two men, who were dismounted, studying a map by the light of an electric lamp. We charged them with the bayonet. The two men were killed and the officer severely wounded. I went to him, and found him a handsome figure of a man, with a face like marble. Lying in a pool of his own blood, he murmured words of which, though I could not understand at first, I gradually gathered

31

the meaning. He said that he was a Pole and a Catholic, and tried to pull from his pocket his rosary and an image of Our Lady and the Infant Jesus. At this sight all my fury died down, and having placed my men at their posts, I went back to him, and made him understand that I too was a Catholic, and that my greatest desire was to comfort his last moments. He seemed to understand, and lifted up his rosary. Seeing what he wanted, I recited a decade, and he answered feebly and more feebly in German, after which he raised the beads to his lips and kissed them several times. Then he handed them to me, and I also kissed them. This seemed to please him. Then I had to go back to my men, so I put his rosary and image in his hands and left him. Next morning, on my way back to the trenches, I found him lying dead just as I had left him" (*Tablet*, December 5th).

An Officer's Testimony.

A writer to the *Evening Standard* stated that he "would rather see our country a German province ten times over than that we should return to Roman Catholicism and idolatry." The remark drew the following testimony from an English officer on active service:—

"May I say how impressed I have been by the extraordinary religion of the people among whom we are campaigning? I have seized every opportunity of attending churches wherever we have been, and of observing the people and their habits.

"I find everywhere a magnificent piety, a religion which guides and fills out the lives of these people. The French soldiers go into the trenches, each with his little medal of Our Lady hung around his neck—they pray aloud in action, not in fear, as we very well know, but with a high courage and a great trust. It is my grief that our poor boys have not the same knowledge to lean on, the same precious comfort in their times of trial and need.

"On All Souls' Day I saw the village curé come out and bless the graves of our poor lads—the graves, mark, of rough Protestant soldiers, decorated with chrysanthemums by the villagers. These poor dead were blessed and called 'the faithful departed,' and wept over and prayed for so strongly and deeply. I think the women of England—the mothers, sisters, and wives of our dead—would have been glad.

"I am not reminded of what Protestants call 'Popery'; here is obviously a people with a full Christianity, a deep piety, a faith infinitely sweet and beautiful and necessary—which we in England have not. There are on roadsides and over doors innumerable shrines and images—but to infer idolatry would be, as Miss Cecilia Loftus writes, utterly 'ignorant and bigoted.'

"What they have seen here will leave its mark on many of our soldiers. My servant, a Wesleyan, an artillery driver, is craving to know more of what he tells me he thinks must be the true faith" (*Evening Standard*, November 16th).

Charity on All Sides.

A Baden paper, quoted in the *Church Times* (November 6th), had the following:—

"An exalted person has visited the tombs of our soldiers fallen in August and September, on the banks of the Oise, and found among many others two large mounds with wreaths of flowers laid upon them. The first bore the inscription: 'Offered by the women of France to the German soldiers, our brothers in Jesus Christ.' A second inscription read: 'For the German soldiers, our brothers in Jesus, dead far away from their country, wept by their families. We pray for them.' German mothers will read, certainly not without emotion, how France treats their sons fallen in the great battle."

Everywhere there has been gratifying generosity and absence of prejudice on the part of non-Catholics. The papers one and all abound with instances of the heroism of priests and nuns, and with sympathetic references to Catholic churches, services, doctrines and customs. The Dean of Exeter sent to Cardinal Mercier, towards restoration of the damaged Cathedral at Malines, the proceeds of a collection made in the Exeter diocese. The Society of SS. Peter and Paul is selling a delightful edition of *The Jackdaw of Rheims* in order to stimulate offerings towards the same object at Rheims. The absence of proselytism among the Belgian refugees is another sign of the times. The general feeling has been voiced by Mr. McEvoy, a Congregationalist minister, at a public meeting held to welcome the refugees: "Don't send tracts and anti-Catholic literature to our Belgian guests: it isn't cricket."

But most touching of all is a story told in the *Jewish World*, and with this instance of true charity we close our collection. The Chief Rabbi of Lyons was attending to some Jewish soldiers when a dying Catholic trooper, mistaking him for a priest, begged him to hold up his crucifix, that he might see it to the last. The Rabbi held the crucifix before the soldier's dying eyes and spoke some words of comfort. In this act of charity, while his hands still held the cross, the Rabbi was killed by a shell from the enemy.

MORE STORIES OF THE WAR

Mrs John Boland [Eileen Boland]

MORE STORIES OF THE WAR

The C.T.S. pamphlet in which *Some Stories of the War* are brought together has proved so acceptable that almost from its first appearance there has been a demand for more of the same kind; hence this second collection. Here and there matter has been included which hardly comes within the strict category of "stories"; but all has a bearing upon the main purpose of the selection, which is to exhibit further instances and proofs of the part being played by the Catholic Faith in connection with the present War. We will open with another note of consolation for our French allies—the

Religious Revival in France.

One of the most remarkable examples of the change effected by the increase of religion in France is afforded by the alteration of the rules governing the admission of chaplains to military hospitals. The Minister for War, M. Millerand, has himself stated the position in an official circular dated October 1, 1914.

"By the terms of the regulations in force, and particularly of the circulars of November 15 and January 24, 1906, ministers of religion specially approved by the military authority to exercise the duties of the ministry in the hospitals under the Department of War, are allowed to enter the hospitals only at the express wish, in each particular instance, of the sick man or of his family."

This meant that the sick man had to sign a formal written declaration before being allowed to receive the visit of a priest, and moreover this formality had to be repeated as often as he wished to see one.

M. Millerand continues: "The Government desires to assure to every soldier the right to practise his religion as he sees fit. I have decided, in consequence, that, throughout the duration of the War, ministers of religion approved of individually by the local military authority will be authorized, without having to prove that they have been specially asked for, to enter the military hospitals daily."

The *Evening Standard* (December 17, 1914) publishes the following from its Paris correspondent:—

"Among the changes wrought by the war in the psychology of the average Parisian none is more noticeable than the revival of religious devotion on the part of the people who hailed with shouts of approval the warfare waged against the Church by MM. Combes and Briand. Necessity makes strange bed-fellows; but, nevertheless, it was somewhat a surprise to find in the crowds that filled all the Paris churches last Sunday—the day set by Cardinal Amette for prayer throughout France—some of the leading Radicals, their heads reverently bowed in supplication, their attitude that of profound faith. The words of Cardinal Amette—who said that while Our Lady of Victories is also Our Lady of Peace, no peace but one worthy of France and her Allies could, and should, be concluded—have found a ready echo in the hearts of Parisians, and the days when the sight of a *curé* provoked ridicule and abuse have, apparently, passed, never to return."

"Being Sunday, we went to the Church of St. Jacques, an old Gothic building, and were greatly struck by the large numbers of French officers and men present at Mass. This was also the case when in Paris a few days previously I was passing 'Notre Dame des Victoires,' and, seeing the crowds going in and out, I myself entered. The spectacle was a memorable one. The great dim aisles were thronged with reverent worshippers, hundreds, even thousands, of candles burning brightly in the obscurity around the altar of Our Lady of Victories. To whatever faith we may belong, it is impossible to fail to be deeply touched by the wave of religious devotion that is at present sweeping over this country and the knowledge that over two thousand priests are fighting in the ranks of the French Army" (*Westminister Gazette*, January 27th).

Describing a Mass in the cathedral at Nancy for the repose of the souls of those who have fallen on the battle-field, the *Times* special correspondent says:—

"In all this there was nothing different from what must always be seen in any country at a time of national mourning. But there was something else. It was a time and an occasion, not only of national mourning, but of national pride. And it was also an occasion and a proof of national unity. In the choir just within the rails of the chancel was the Prefect of Meurthe and Moselle. To an Englishman that may not sound in any way remarkable. But the French congregation knew what his presence there meant. It is probably the first time for at least fifteen years that a Prefect, wearing his official uniform, has taken part in a religious service. That is what has been done for France by the war and the sacrifice of its soldiers' lives."

The Soldier-priests.

Writing in the *Daily Chronicle* (February 10th) Mr. Philip Gibbs says:—

"The priest-soldier in France is a spiritual influence among his comrades, so that they fight with nobler motives than that of blood-lust.… A young priest who says his prayers before lying down on his straw mattress or in the mud of his trench puts a check upon blasphemy, and his fellows—anti-clericals perhaps in the old days, or frank materialists—watch him curiously, and are thoughtful after their watchfulness. It is easy to see that he is eager to give up his life as a sacrifice to the God of his faith. His courage has something supernatural in it, and he is careless of death."

"We are very ready," the *Gaulois* says, "to speak ill of the Jesuits, and to charge them with all sorts of misdemeanours, and with every kind of intrigue. This is how they have been intriguing, and the nature of their misdeeds: 'Of 502 Jesuits who became French soldiers when war was declared, forty-two have been killed by the enemy, ten are reported "missing," nineteen are prisoners of war, six have received the Cross of the Legion of Honour, six have received the Medaille Militaire, one has received the Russian Cross of St. George, and another the Medaille des Epidémies. Finally, thirty of these Jesuits have been mentioned in dispatches [cités à l'ordre du jour]'" (*Westminster Gazette*, July 13th).

Another Priest-hero.

The story of the Abbé Armand, in the 14th Battalion of the Chasseurs Alpins, is that of a hero. A simple man, he used to open his heart to his rough comrades, and often in the trenches, under shell fire, he would recite the Psalms in a clear voice, so that they could hear him. On November 17th, to the south of Ypres, his company was selected to hold a dangerous position, swept by the heavy guns of the Germans and near the enemy's trenches. All day until the evening the priest and his comrades stayed there, raked by a hideous shell fire. At last nearly all the men were killed, and on his side of the emplacement the Abbé Armand was left with only two men alive. He signalled the fact to those below by raising three fingers, but shortly afterwards a bullet struck him so that he fell and another hit him in the stomach. It was impossible to send help to him at the time, and he died half an hour later on the tumulus, surrounded by the dead bodies of his comrades. They buried him up there, and that night his loss was mourned, not without tears, by many rough soldiers who had loved the man for his cheeriness, and honoured him for the simple faith which seemed to put a glamour about the mud-stained uniform of a soldier of France.

The Abbé Bertrand, vicar of St. Germain de Coulamer, was mobilized on the outbreak of war, and for his gallantry in the field promoted successively to the ranks of sergeant, sergeant-major, sub-lieutenant, and lieutenant. He fell on November 4th, at the battle of Audrechy, leading his men to the assault. A few days before his death he wrote: "I always look upon this war as an expiation, and I am proud to be a victim." And again: "Oh, how cold the rain is, and how severe the weather! For our faith in France I have offered God to let me be wet and soaked to the very bones."

How Father Finn Died.

The first British chaplain to fall at the post of duty was Father Finn, of the Middlesbrough diocese, whose heroic death in the Dardanelles operations is thus recorded in the *Daily News* (June 7th):—

"The losses sustained by the Dublins and King's Own Scottish Borderers in the Dardanelles have been greatly felt by the many friends of these two regiments in Cairo, where they did garrison duty some five or six years ago, but perhaps no death has been more keenly felt than that of Father Finn, the Roman Catholic chaplain, who was so well liked in English circles here.

"Father Finn was one of the first to give his life in the landing at Sedd-ul-Bahr. In answer to the appeals that were made to him not to leave the ship, he replied, 'A priest's place is beside the dying soldier,' whereupon he stepped on to the gangway, immediately receiving a bullet through the chest. Undeterred, he made his way across the lighters, receiving another bullet in the thigh, and still another in the leg. By the time he reached the beach he was literally riddled with bullets, but in spite of the great pain he must have been suffering he heroically went about his duties, giving consolation to the dying troops. It was while he was in the act of attending to the spiritual requirements of one of his men that the priest's head was shattered by shrapnel."

A noble sense of duty; and a fine end. May he rest in peace!

A German Priest's Bravery.

T.P.'s Journal of Great Deeds relates the following story of priestly courage in the enemy's lines:—

"I went to occupy a trench from which the Germans had lately been evicted. It was quite dark, and on entering the trench at the head of my party I heard some one talking in a low voice. I crept forward as quietly as I could, and saw what I imagined must be a doctor supporting the head of a wounded man. I called upon him to surrender, and he held up a crucifix towards me, so I knew he must be a priest. The priest was giving absolution to a dying Bavarian, who expired a few minutes later. I went up to the priest, who, however, could not understand English or French. I know very little German—only a few words in fact; so we fell back on Latin, in which tongue we held a short and very halting conversation. As far as I could make out, he said that the Germans were suffering much from sickness, and he disliked the Prussians most cordially. Eventually I allowed him to return to the German trenches, which I expect and hope that he reached in safety. The courage of the German priest in remaining to give absolution to his dying countrymen surpasses anything I have heard myself in the course of the present war, as he must have known that he would fall into the hands not of British soldiers, who might possibly have respected his calling, but into those of men who must have been represented to him as barbarous savages."

A Protestant's Tribute.

The following letter from a Protestant soldier at the front, Driver F. J. Collinson, appeared in the *Stratford Express* for June 12th:—

"Dear Sir,—As you granted me my wish by inserting my last letter in the *Stratford Express*, I trust that this letter may be of some interest to you. My sole idea in writing this is to try and impress people at home how faithful the Roman Catholic priests are to their duty. Although I have been brought up as a strict Protestant, I must plainly express that I have never seen or heard of such heroism as these abbés show. They practically fight amongst themselves to be able to go into the first line of trenches, and when the wounded are put in our ambulance and are beyond aid the priests will suffer any inconvenience to be able to pray by their side while we are tearing along on our errand of mercy. They come for a few days' rest from the trenches, and, whenever they meet me, always a cheerful and brave phrase comes from their lips. Most of them are in soldier's clothes, and by the manly way they work one would never think that they held such a high rank in private life. I have never seen one of them show any signs of weariness. When I have a puncture or engine trouble they are always the first to have their hands black. My opinion of them is more than I can express. While writing this there are two of them washing a bloody ambulance down, with coats off and buckets in hand. One of them, being an old man, is puffing and blowing, yet he is singing a song which I cannot understand. While all this is going on there is the boom, boom, boom of the heavy artillery, the ping of the rifle, and three men are manning a mitrailleuse on a Taube which is hovering over the lines. Yet these brave men work day by day without a flinch, or, when they are hurt, without a cry or a curse. I trust that this letter will not bore you, but my opinion of the Roman Catholic priest will always be of the highest, although my religion will never change from Protestant."

Three Brave Nuns.

Mr. Philip Gibbs, in the *Daily Chronicle* for January 29th, tells the story of Sister Gabrielle, a nun of St. Vincent of Paul.

"In the town of Clermont-en-Argonne she refused to leave when the wounded had been evacuated and the inhabitants had fled before the enemy, and, with three other nuns, remained in her convent with 42 old people who could not be removed. The town became a flaming torch about her, and when the Germans entered they pillaged her convent and terrified the helpless old creatures, until the resolution of Sister Gabrielle, and the utter fearlessness of her spirit, won the respect of a German officer, who saved the house from the fire and from the soldiery. At one moment death seemed very close to them, for a German soldier was accidentally wounded by a splinter from a burning beam, and his comrades swore that he had been fired upon by some one in the convent. A hostage was taken, but once again Sister Gabrielle's influence saved the situation, and the German officer kept his word that no harm should befall her people."

Under the title of "Unknown Heroes," a special correspondent of *Le Petit Marseillais* includes Sister St. Louis.

"Before setting up her small hospital in the backyard of a Glonville farmhouse, she went over all the neighbouring battlefields, with help for the wounded and words of comfort for the dying. When her improvised hospital was just arranged the enemy presented himself. The inhabitants who had not already taken to flight were panic-stricken, for the soldiery shouted, drank, and robbed wherever there were spoils or liquor. There were only women, children, and old men to stop the way. The Germans began to fix bayonets, and to harry the terrorized weaklings, who fled from house to house in the fruitless attempt to find hiding-places. At last the wretched people were 'rounded-up,' as it were, at one end of the townlet. The farm blocked their further progress.

In the backyard the Sister had arranged beds for her wounded. As there was absolutely no way of getting round the buildings, the terrified people pushed in, by the house door, like a flock of sheep through a gap when flying before the burning of a field. The poor things all believed that their last hour had struck! The Sister's first care was to soothe her visitors, as far as that was possible. When they had recovered some courage and self-possession she ordered them all to lie down. Her tone was firm and full of authority. She added '*I* will go and meet them!'

"Sister St. Louis had nothing but the cross of her order, and her position as head of the little make-shift hospital, to give her authority; but she stepped into the road, and faced five or six reeling soldiers, who were coming out of a small grocery shop, which they had entirely pillaged. The men were unshaven, dirty, and ragged, as well as drunk, and they made for the door of the farm, with the evident intention of going in there.

"'Summon your officer here,' the Sister ordered. The men stood still at this unlooked-for command, hesitated a moment, then made off—without a word to her! They had hardly gone, when other soldiers came towards the doorway, but Sister St. Louis barred the passage, and twice, or thrice, she succeeded in turning off intruders. A passing officer saw her keeping guard, and asked her to explain why she was refusing his soldiers admittance. The brave nun, though certainly agitated, was not afraid; and she told him, in few words, exactly how matters stood, and asked him to send a picket to guard the hospital.

"The officer may have been suspicious, or, perhaps, he was only curious. In any case, he dismounted, and went through to the farmyard. Some of the refugees were crying. When he saw the frightened people he turned to the Sister, saying: 'As your sick folk are in such good health you shall take care of *our* wounded.'

"'Gladly,' answered Sister St. Louis, 'but on condition that I may

45

also nurse the French wounded, and that none of the people who took refuge here shall be in any manner molested by your men.'

"The officer consented; and in this way a good portion of Glonville's inhabitants escaped many of the horrors which have only too often marked the German occupation of French territory" (*Universe*, March 26th).

In one of the recent French "Orders of the Day" occurs the following testimony to the devotion of a nun;—

"Sister Hippolyte, Superior of the Sisters of the Mixed Hospital at Baccarat, has given the finest example of courage and self-sacrifice by remaining at the head of her staff to care for the wounded received at the hospital during the bombardment and occupation of the town in August and September" (*Tablet*, February 20th).

Queen Alexandra and the Sisters.

Queen Alexandra has addressed the following autotograph letter to the Lady Superior of the hospital at Béthune, which is one of many under the guidance of the Franciscan Sisters:—

"Madame la Supérieure,

"I have learned through Dr. Martin of your noble and heroic devotion to our brave and unfortunate wounded soldiers, and it is with a heart full of gratitude that I beg you to accept my warmest thanks. I pray that God may reward you for the angelic care which you have lavished on our poor soldiers, and I shall never forget that it is to you, Madam, and to your Sisters that they undoubtedly owe their life and the restoration of their health.

"I beg you, Madam, to accept the assurance of my highest esteem" (*Times*, February 16th).

Mr. Ian Malcolm, M.P., tells the following story of

Mass Under Fire.

"In the last five days there have been five desperate street fights outside our hospital. The Sisters found bullets in their beds and eight shells fell on their convent. The fury of the cannonading was maddening.

"Last Friday, a soldier-priest got leave to come and say Mass in the chapel attached to the hospital. Another priest from the Red Cross assisted him as a server.

" 'Come along, Sister,' said the soldier, 'we haven't time for long meditations this morning; our moments are very precious.' So we got everything ready and Mass began: the server's responses were entirely drowned by the noise of the guns outside.... He was really a brave young fellow, but very pale, I thought, and rather absent-minded perhaps. No doubt he could not help following the course of the battle, even on his knees. We reached the Offertory...a grinding crash fell upon the chapel...a fearful explosion shook the hospital to its base...a long, long moan of anguish followed as four poor officers were carried away on stretchers. The priest, who had paused for a moment, went on with his prayers, but his server seemed turned to stone as he knelt huddled against the wall, saying no responses and ringing no bell. Our Superior made signs to him, but they had no effect at all. The Sisters knelt down to receive their Communion, when another shell burst right over us, smashing every window in the place. This time it fell just outside the west end door. In the heart of this hell the Sisters made their Communion...but nothing could rouse our server from his trance.

"When he came to himself, the Superior said: 'But, my dear Father, you quite forgot the ablutions; you must be very distraught this morning.'

" 'Forgive me, Mother,' he answered, 'I believe I was mummified.' And perhaps he was, for the moment; but since then he has won the much-coveted medal for bravery in the field" (*Church Times*, April 30th).

Mass for the Enemy Dead.

Here is an account of another Mass under fire, with the strange and almost paradoxical contrast presented by a French priest-officer whose military duty obliges him to slay the enemy, and who immediately afterwards is impelled by Christian charity to offer Mass for their eternal repose.

"A story is told of how a captain of artillery, who in peace time fills the *rôle* of *curé*, said Mass among the ruins of a church from which his battery had just expelled the enemy, after putting one of their batteries out of action.

"The action began by a rush of French colonial troops under a murderous machine-gun fire. They made a dash for twenty yards, dropped, rose again—not all of them, alas!—and went forward afresh. It was necessary to take a point of great strategical importance, and things were going rather badly, when suddenly a battery of 75's arrived at full gallop. It was commanded by a gigantic captain of almost ferocious mien—certainly not the kind of man to trifle with.

"He climbed into a tree, and came down after three minutes' observation. Then he indicated the range for his battery, and it started work, with the result that two German batteries were silenced in quick time. Their fire ceased as if by magic, and the colonials made rapid progress, none of them biting the dust now.

"The French battery limbered up, and drove into what remained of the village in front. The horses were once more tethered, and the gunners, after carefully brushing themselves, vanished into a ruined grange.

"Here a strange spectacle presented itself. A stone had been placed upon some empty cartridge-boxes, and the artillery captain said Mass. The captain's three stripes were scarcely hidden by the *curé*'s priestly robe.

"Nothing was left out of the service. In a sermon the *curé*-captain told his listeners first of all to pray for all on behalf of whom he was going to say Mass. 'I recommend in particular for your prayers the German artillerymen whom we have just destroyed,' he said. The *De Profundis* followed. All round the village German 'marmites' were exploding while the captain raised his hand for the *Benedicat vos!*

"One cannot adequately describe the impression of this Mass, said to an accompaniment of machine gun fire, the effect of this Credo chanted by the soldiers in the midst of the roar of the cannon; and the sight of this priest, who was giving his blessing but a few moments after having sent to another world over 100 Germans with the fire of his battery" (*Daily Chronicle*, February 24th).

Piety in the Trenches.

"On the feast of All Saints last November, while the Germans were doing their utmost to effect the destruction of churches, a little group of soldiers in one of the trenches near Chalon-sur-Marne were proving that, as in the humble stable of Bethlehem, the love and devotion of human hearts can replace fine architecture. Mass having been said in a neighbouring church by a priest-infirmarian (one, indeed, who had supplied at Westminster Cathedral during the summer vacation of 1912), the Pyx containing the Sacred Host was carried into a corner of the trench in order that some officers and men who were absent might receive Holy Communion the next day; and there, throughout the day and night, incessant devotion was offered up to Our Lord in the Blessed Sacrament by the soldiers on duty" (*Westminster Cathedral Chronicle*, February 1915).

The Rosary.

The following is surely a touching proof of the piety of the French soldiers in the firing line, as well as of the old saw that necessity is the mother of invention. It is taken from a letter by the Abbé Jarraud, a professor at the school of Notre Dame at Issoudun, who has been for four months with the ambulance near the Grand Couronné of Nancy: "At the Presbytery of Varangéville I saw and venerated a rosary made of string, which was made in the trenches by a young soldier of the —— Regiment of the Line, the knots nicely spaced, representing exactly the Pater and Ave beads. This edifying rosary is nearly worn out, for it has seen much service every day of the defence of Couronné. 'All the men of the section passed it on from one to another to say a Hail Mary,' said the brave soldier, very simply, who came to the *curé* to ask in exchange for it a strong rosary to use on the Northern frontier" (*Tablet*, February 13th).

"A glowing tribute to the piety of the Breton soldiers has been written by one of the chaplains to the Archbishop of Rennes. He tells how they flock to the churches and to the sacraments and say the Rosary together in the trenches. By way of illustration he describes the following little incident which happened in the trenches: The commanding officer of the neighbouring village one day saw one of the soldiers in the trenches saying his Rosary. 'Do you say it because you are afraid?' he asked. 'No, mon Colonel,' replied the soldier, 'but because it helps me.' 'That's right,' said the colonel; 'let's say it together.' And with this he took out his beads and began to say them with the soldier. The example was infectious; one after another the men did the same, and soon the whole trench was saying the Rosary together" (*Cork Examiner*, May 15th).

A Christmas Mass.

The following picture of a midnight Mass, celebrated in the war zone to usher in the Christmas of 1914, is taken from the *Month* (June 1915). It is a French Jesuit who writes:—

"I arranged with our Colonel to say a midnight Mass for those who could get out of the trenches. We fixed on a hamlet well to the front, deserted by its inhabitants and shelled to pieces. Soon the men returning from the trenches appeared, and they could hardly believe their ears when I told them they should have Mass. At once confessions began, one in a cave, another in a room open to all the winds, another in the road. The Colonel took me to the room where the Mass was to be said, when word came that a German attack was expected, and many of the soldiers would have to return at once. I consoled them by promising to bring them Holy Communion afterwards. At midnight I began; there were a few artificial flowers on my altar found by a soldier in a house close by. We could not sing; indeed had to take great care to make no noise at all, so close were we to the enemy; all who were present had their arms with them ready to leave at the sound of alarm. After the Mass I took the remaining Hosts, but was unable to carry them into the trenches on account of the expected attack. So I clasped the Blessed Sacrament to my breast and lay down on some straw in a cave, by the side of some officers. It was Christmas night, and the Child Jesus lay on the straw of Bethlehem; nothing could happen to us that night at least. And so I fell asleep, meditating upon Bethlehem, and thanking Him for this midnight Mass that had had no music but the thundering of the guns. At six o'clock I was on foot again towards the nearest village, to say my second and third Mass."

The Munsters' Chaplain.

The *Daily Mail* prints a letter written home from the front by a sergeant-major of the 2nd Royal Munster Fusiliers, in the course of which he says:—

"We have a priest attached to the battalion, Father Gleeson, a Thurles man. He said Mass for us on Christmas Day actually in the firing line! Where he had his little altar was peppered with bullets. He is a grand priest, and knows no fear. He is never finished doing all in his power for every one, even those who are not of the same religion. It is only natural that a Tipperary man should be brave. He is here now, only fifty yards from the trenches, with some neat crosses which he made himself to place over a few of our brave Fusiliers who died last night.

"Nothing gives him greater pleasure than saying a Mass in the open, in cold and wet, or hearing confessions in some old barn that has been half-blown away by German shell fire. He even went to the little church near the village where we are and took two statues out of it. Everything in it was blown to atoms except the altar."

A further tribute—one of many, to this courageous chaplain, says:—

"There is not a braver man on the field than Father Gleeson, our chaplain. A soldier gets forty-eight hours' work and then rest. Father Gleeson never gets rest, and seems never to sleep. He is a sheer knock-out. He marches with the men, billets with them, gets the same shower of bullets, shell, or shrapnel, yet the Huns have never, thank God, scored a hit off him. God gave him to the Munsters, and God preserves him to them. His blessing is for everybody, and many a Protestant has asked for it, and got it."

What the Munsters think of Father Gleeson is reflected back in what Father Gleeson thinks of them. Viewing their faith and constancy, he writes of his men: "The Munster boys are a downright credit to us all."

In a German Prison-camp.

Father Crotty, O.P., describes an impressive scene in one of the prison-camps in Germany, when the Irish Catholics among the prisoners organized a procession through the camp in honour of Our Lady:—

"Last Sunday we had the procession through the camp in honour of Our Blessed Lady. The crucifix was borne in front by Rev. Brother Warren, who was captured in Ghent and brought in here with some other prisoners. Two of the prisoners acted as acolytes and accompanied the cross-bearer. After these came six Irishmen, the tallest of the 2,500, bearing on their shoulders a platform on which was the statue of Our Blessed Lady. The season of the year and the rich soil of the Lahn Valley furnished us with flowers, which we formed into bouquets to adorn the 'Image of our Queen.' It was a grand sight to behold the long line of Irishmen marching eight abreast, through the camp, singing hymns to Mary and reciting the Holy Rosary. On our arrival at a large square we halted. A sermon was then delivered, and before we began again to march the whole assembly sang with great fervour the hymn, 'Faith of our Fathers.' At the last stanza the procession started once more, and those of the crowd who could enter came into the chapel where we sang the Litany of Loreto. Before concluding the devotions the prayer of the Pope for peace was recited, and to further honour the Mother of God all pronounced after me the form of a pledge which nearly all of them took for life" (*Cork Examiner*, May 27th).

An Officer's Conversion.

On the evening of the Feast of All Saints, 1914, a young officer called at a convent in Westminster and asked for instruction. This was his story. He came of a Protestant family but he had one Catholic friend who had spoken to him of the Catholic religion as the only religion to die in. He was up in London for the day and was to rejoin his regiment that night. They were to go to the front two days later. He had, he said, a presentiment that he should never return, and he had made up his mind to become a Catholic. He had no notion how to set about it, but finding that a man working in the place where he stayed in town was a Catholic, F. asked his advice, and was taken by him to the convent. On the way—so sure was he of his intentions—he erased "Church of England" from his identification disc and scratched "R.C." beside it. When he arrived at the convent it was already six o'clock, and his train left at 8.30, so Sister N., hearing his story, took him at once to a priest at Westminster Cathedral, who instructed him, prepared him for confession, and gave him conditional baptism. "Thank God," said F., when the ceremony was over, "now if I'm hit I can call a priest." That night he told his fellow-officers of his reception into the Church, and for the next two days he had to stand a good deal of chaff; for he had never been considered a serious-minded man, and this apparently sudden turn to religion in a boy of twenty-one bewildered his friends.

On November 4th he went to the front, and we have no record of his first weeks of Catholic life. From December 3rd we have his diary. Here are extracts from the entries:—

"December 4th. Go to Confession, Holy Communion [this was his first Communion] and Mass in morning."

"December 10th. Usual parade in morning. Feeling very fed-up and unhappy, don't know why. Parade 7.30 to go back."

There is no entry for the 11th. On the 12th he lifted his head above the trench and was shot through the brain by a sniper. Death was instantaneous. Some days later the following letter, marked "To be sent after death," reached his friend. It was written on December 3rd, the day before his first Communion.

"I have been talking to a R.C. priest and I feel much the better for it. If you ever get this you will know I am gone to a better place. Live a pious life and if I have gone to the right place you will join me later on. It is very hard to write a letter that won't be delivered till after you're gone. Good-bye and God bless you and keep you.—F."

Immunity of the Crucifix.

An officer, writing to the Notre Dame High School, Glasgow, says:—

"I wish you could see some of the pictures I have seen. Then indeed you would pray—not only for those out here, but also to thank God that Britain has been spared such scenes. The other week I was in a village that had suffered heavily from shell fire. There was not a single house standing intact, and only a few that were not heaps of bricks. And once they were homes. I visited the remains of the church. Here and there were banners—or rather what had been banners. The altar a ruin—the tabernacle open; but standing—triumphant almost—uninjured amidst the *débris* was the crucifix of the Calvary. The statue of Our Lady and that of her divine Son were alone uninjured, although surrounded by marks of burst shells. Outside the church, too, the crucifix was uninjured. I was told that it was a common thing for the crucifix alone to escape injury."

The official "Eye Witness" thus describes, on March 26th, the *débris* of a French village:—

"The appearance of the village itself suggests the havoc wrought by an earthquake, for the place is one huge rubbish-heap; it is almost impossible to distinguish the streets amongst the rubble and bricks which have been hurled across and obliterated them. Here and there portions of houses are still standing, but these are few and far between and are dangerous to enter on account of falling tiles and tottering walls. In the churchyard the very dead have been uprooted, only to be buried again under masonry which has fallen from the church, and crosses from the heads of the tombs lie scattered in all directions. The sole thing in the cemetery that has escaped damage is a wooden crucifix still erect amid the medley of overturned graves. There is another large crucifix still standing at the cross-roads at the north end of the village, and at the time our troops entered a dead German soldier was lying at its foot."

The same writer had previously (March 5th) described the condition of the church at Messines:—

"The church contained a very fine oak screen, in the centre of which was a life-size plaster crucifix. When the British evacuated the place on October 31st the German shells had set alight to the woodwork, which was completely burnt, and everything in the church destroyed, with the sole exception of the crucifix, which was not touched."

Private T. Conroy, of the R.I. Fusiliers, writes:—

"In one place not far from the firing line there is Confession and Communion every morning by an English priest. The church itself has its steeple blown away and other parts damaged, but a big crucifix of our Lord on the Cross, hanging on the outside wall, is not touched at all; the shells are constantly falling about the place, yet the priest goes on with Mass just the same as if nothing was wrong at all" (*Tablet*, March 20th).

"In this war of desecration and sacrilege, of pillaged churches, not one, but many, stories centre round holy things. One tells of a band of Uhlan foragers who came upon a church and decided to loot it. While at their work, one trooper wagered another that he would destroy the stately crucifix that stood upon the altar. The bet was accepted, and the Uhlan sprang quickly upon the altar and wrenched at the sacred emblem. He could not move it, and he exerted more and more strength, but fruitlessly. Then, in a final burst of savagery, he swung a blow at the crucifix and missed; to fall from the altar a second later with his ankle badly fractured. It is curious, indeed, how not only a crucifix, but a multitude of crucifixes have escaped injury in the fighting, though the churches in which they stand have fallen about them in ruin. 'A Catholic church had suffered somewhat from artillery fire, and the walls and roof had been completely demolished, but the notable feature was that the altar, even to the floral decorations and candles, was quite intact.' That is contained in a letter from Private Welsh, of the Irish Rifles. It is a passage that occurs in many letters. Private D. Singleton, of the East Lancs, found this singular immunity almost startling. 'The most wonderful thing to me is that let into two of the walls are images of Christ, and they are the only walls standing (he writes). It is simply marvellous how some of these images have escaped injury when the remainder of the building has been wrecked.'" (*T.P.'s Journal of Great Deeds*).

Catholic V.C.s.

Catholics are well represented among the winners of the Victoria Cross for acts of conspicuous personal gallantry. At least half a dozen names can be cited, and there may be others. Stonyhurst College is proud of the V.C. awarded to one of its "old boys," Lieut. M. J. Dease; humbler Catholic schools in England and Ireland are no less proud of having educated the heroes of the rank and file who now wear this coveted distinction.

Sergeant Michael O'Leary's exploit has been written about, and his praises sung, all over the British Empire. The official record in the *London Gazette* is eloquent of his courage in its own simple terms:—

"For conspicuous bravery at Cuinchy on February 1, 1915, when forming one of the storming party which advanced against the enemy's barricades he rushed to the front and himself killed five Germans who were holding the first barricade, after which he attacked a second barricade, about 60 yards further on, which he captured after killing three of the enemy and making prisoners of two more. Lance-Corporal O'Leary thus practically captured the enemy's position by himself, and prevented the rest of the attacking party from being fired upon."

Sergeant O'Leary (he earned swift promotion by his great deed) is an Irish Guardsman, and a native of Co. Cork. He is the first soldier of the Irish Guards to win the Cross.

Lance-Corporal Dwyer, the youngest V.C. in the army (he enlisted at sixteen), saved a trench single-handed, by leaping upon the parapet and engaging the approaching enemy with hand-grenades, keeping them at bay until supports arrived.

Corporal Holmes, a Bermondsey Catholic, has received the French Military Medal in addition to the Victoria Cross. The dispatch recording his bravery at Le Cateau, on August 26th, states that he "carried a wounded officer out of the trenches under a heavy fire, and later assisted to drive a gun out of action by taking the place of the driver, who had been wounded." Corporal Holmes was himself seriously wounded, and was for several weeks an in-patient at English military hospitals.

Drummer Lance-Corporal William Kenny, of the Gordon Highlanders, a native of Co. Wicklow, was awarded the V.C. for conspicuous bravery on October 23rd, near Ypres, in rescuing wounded men on five occasions under very heavy fire, in the most fearless manner, and for twice previously saving machine guns by carrying them out of action. On numerous occasions also Lance-Corporal Kenny conveyed urgent messages under very dangerous circumstances over fire-swept ground.

Another Catholic, Sergeant John Hogan, of the 2nd Manchesters, earned the Cross for conspicuous bravery near

Festubert on October 29th, when he and a young officer (Lieut. J. Leach, also decorated as V.C.) recovered a trench by themselves, killing or wounding ten of the enemy, and making sixteen prisoners.

BACKGROUND

These booklets come from the first year of the Great War, when British involvement was mostly limited to the men of the Regular Army and the Territorial Force. Wartime volunteers ("Kitchener's Armies") did not reach the front line until 1916. Many of the stories concern French clergy in uniform; the anti-clerical government there refused to exempt priests from military service, and so many fought in the trenches. Their witness did something to dissolve anti-clerical prejudice. Other stories involve atrocities perpetrated by German troops in Belgium, some against priests and nuns. It used to be fashionable to dismiss these as wartime propaganda; but there is good evidence that the German Army pursued a deliberate policy of terror with the aim of discouraging resistance amongst the civilian population. Belgium was famously the most devout Catholic country in Europe; religious would have been obvious and visible targets. That being said, other stories here show the Germans acting as fellow-Christians.

CTS ONEFIFTIES